T0247338

Poem for the End of Time and Other Poems

NOELLE KOCOT

POEM FOR THE END OF TIME AND OTHER POEMS

WAVE BOOKS

SEATTLE/NEW YORK

Published by Wave Books www.wavepoetry.com

Wave Books titles are distributed to the trade by Consortium Book Sales
and Distribution, 1045 Westgate Drive, St. Paul, Minnesota 55114

Library of Congress Cataloging-in-Publication Data
    Kocot, Noelle.
    Poem for the end of time and other poems /
    Noelle Kocot.— 1st ed.
        p. cm.
    ISBN 1-933517-01-8 (pbk. : alk. paper)
    ISBN 1-933517-05-0 (alk. paper)
    I. Title.
    PS3611.036P64 2006
    813'.6—dc22   2005023746

The author wishes to thank the following publications, in which several
of these poems first appeared: *Alaska Quarterly Review, Conduit,
The Iowa Review, LUNGFULL!,* and *New American Writing.*

Designed by Quemadura, and printed in the United States
of America on acid-free, recycled paper

9 8 7 6 5 4 3 2 1

First Edition

Wave Books 001

CONTENTS

He wept. **JOHN 11:35**

Poem for the End of Time and Other Poems

SONG

An orange radio is all I need
To keep me in green seas

I slip between the corners of the wind
And drink to remember you.

Be the skin on my lap
As I kneel once again upon your absence.

An orange radio, green seas . . .

And for that which is not said
And for that which is already said

I lay down my head
To the very end of my silence

To the very end of my silence
I lay down my head.

LITHIUM

I have my finger on the pulse of something.
My mind is a sea that eats me,
The fidgety harmony of two trains passing.
A car bathes in its own blueness,
The moon is a yolk that beyolks us,
While I am daring to fault the ergonomics of destiny.
And the helpless word propels itself through the inkjets,
The word that dashes itself against the rocks like an actor.

And affliction cannot speak to non-affliction,
Counting its wounds on the abacus of time.
I know what it is to mourn,
And to breathe bliss into the wormhole of the senses,
And that I must disabuse myself of the lion's share of
    who-knows-where
And the whirring of new grasses on the rainy side of spring.

I AM LIKE A DESERT OWL, AN OWL AMONG THE RUINS

The alpha You. The omega You.
My grandmother's ghost, its girlish snafu
Basking in the waters of urgency.

But I want the coolness of snow.
I want pairs of hands that speak to me cleanly,
Sutras to resuscitate what reigns

Over warped celluloid and heirlooms I can't touch.
There are no family photographs.
Once I was ordinary.

I rattled around with arms, with legs,
With a damp remembering that served me well.
Then, a little sleep, a little slumber,

A little folding of the hands to rest.
I asked myself, don't you just love it?
And then, why don't you just love it?

And then, from what grace have I fallen?
Am I Sisyphus with his mute rock
Unsettling the topsoil, dissolved now

Into brandied battle shouts and pages that breathe like people?
There are hazards here, more so than before
The Furies struck and scarved the white night sifting

The bright waterlights blinking
And grieving over a mash of ice.
Like them, I wanted only to die, moon-dark, blessed,

Poised beneath the driest arrows of my suffering,
Far from the flocks of burning, singing gulls,
Face to face with the God of my childhood.

THE NOWHERE PARADE

Love soils at the drip of a tendon
And blank is nothing in the roundesphere.

H. attacks the great totems of passion,
And now we annul the wholly there
Until our sextants darken remarkable.

I'd like to lie in the cool grass
With my haggard nostrums.
It would be like fire in the crossroads;
A fuschia archaeopteryx would eat my bones.

Love soils, see how easy?
Slender quietness, transubstantiating octave,
What happened to your velocity
On this rainy zero?

OUR DAYS ARE NUMBERED

You wanted to concoct a monody
On a dead-end highway
In an impossible springtime.

Your gravity, your counter-hell
Wreaked the restless angles of your mind.
You turned back into letters

As you brought to yoke the ancient nothingness
In the wind of myth,
In a flock of time,

And your thirsty mirrors
Lynched the shadow of a bridesmaid.
I've told this to no one else,

How the traces of your blond
Preside over a thimble full of light,
How a crack in the fetid sky veers

Into the molting radiance of a gun
Cocked toward the skin of heaven—
Knowing that in one blurred instant

Some architectural speck will fit itself
Into the puzzle of antique indiscretions
Threaded through a buttonhole in your shirt.

We have reached a place where everything
Can be signed away while the hours
Sprint by on the glinting legs of cranes.

POSTLUDE

Surface of the limit.
Index of panic.
My signature in a bucket.

The twilight hung, an asterisk
Above the barefoot knells
While I sang to you,
I can't iron out the chaoses
Under an alcoholic flame.

A phone was swaying underwater.
I craved a round ashtray.
New profundities espoused a relic
Brimming on the outskirts of
        I love you
          LOve you
           luv u
Shearing my equidistant pedals.

Mystic agencies. Elysian slobber.
Pulverize my tortoiseshell into the next solar system.
Gravity hissed and gravity hissed

Like being in the same room together.

IN SICKNESS

You hide for your life in aporias
Counting the skies,
Blessing the blessed,

Hide in the horse-drawn mindset
Of one year cleaving to the next
In shrill antiphony.

Poaching the drama,
Your finger cries *wee wee wee*
Your oars dig numb into solace

Your loops swallow themselves
Until they are younger loops
While your dark night bridges you fluently.

You hide in the awning of a candle
Calling someone Meridian
Calling someone the "rhombus of desire"

While a woman washes your back.
You complain—no love songs,
And on the menu there is alligator

Which makes your breath smell.
But there are also dandelions
And the threat of winter trees

The unflux of driven stars
This furnace of *And*.

IS IT DREAMIER WHERE YOU ARE?

I walk among the hidden vestibules
On a perfectly flawed mission of getting older.

Soft white words are emblazoned on the sky.
To guide me? No, the thrashing of a dispirited

Angel, a trail of stones strangled
In the grassy wind. My gradecard

Salutes the falsehood of this planet.
My errors are silver in the twilight.

I truly intended to unravel the stories
That children have carved on soap,

Penumbra of ancestries properly wired,
While someone sings on a lawn chair

Directions for my departure:
Jump through this door,

Our collective sadness is buzzing with opportunity,
Ten thousand bees lighting on ice.

TU FU

Softly bleats the irony on the table.
Softly bleats the
I am too scheduled to include myself.
Joe I am orangutan of this life
Swishing bananas across the angry netting.
Someone named Iris eats with me every night.
She eats with me and knows I am a non-living thing.
She eats bananas, sometimes coffee, sometimes.
Sometimes I give meaning to what is happening.
I attach large myths to my daily life.
I am a novel and a poem and an epic.
I sing songs to myself in the dark.
I sing songs to myself in the daytime.
The first line of every song hurts me.
Poor, I am not an ancient Chinese poet
Living in a metaphorical hut, reading Tu Fu.

OASIS

When a beautiful woman cuts herself
In a movie, tinsel falls from the universe.
And when you ask someone if I am beautiful,
You don't ask to affirm me, but to affirm
Your own conjecture that I might be
As beautiful as you once thought.
In the playground of our forgetfulness,
A shade guides us back to the berm

Of the road, away from the yellow line,
And you know the exact right thing to say
In order that we salvage our sexy lies
Flying into our beautiful tomorrows
Like the curtains of a hero. And what
Do you suppose the weather will be like then?

I'M NOT FIGHTING IT.
BUT IT ISN'T DOING ME ANY GOOD.

Neural white in welkin blue.
Traumatic acceptance in the blowing wind.
Too much inhaling deeply within the legal limit.
Closing one's eyes in deference to the magma
Of wedding rings, I do not swagger beyond the solstice.
I want to hear the song of the twanging firmament,
A destiny whose entrails are a method.
There are artichokes boiling on the stove,
A picture being hung,
A reversal of all known convictions in the semi-dark terrain.
I watch other people's little windfalls
In the bright passage of days.
They fall beyond the precinct of chipped hands.
They fall beyond the trap door where love is burning.

MY DEVILISH ANCESTORS
SKIRT ME ON THE SLY

My devilish ancestors skirt me on the sly.
O what is real? A hiss darkens
The telephone. Night reasons.
An aria of nails spells OUT
Over cars blossoming their ha-ha's.
For years now I barely return.
But you, little dervish, eat the rich
Despite the cannon pointed against you.
Flexed under each shoveling
You stand. Amen. Laughing hair.

My devilish ancestors skirt me on the sly.
O what is real? God. Damn.

ODE TO MY CAT EUCLID

Mackerel sky above my dinner bell,
A chicken flies across the sun.
A tail floats around a corner in smoothest luxury.
Loving fool, you are no serf among my kingdom.
Piano keys breathe onto your lamp
As gravity wraps its vectors around your bones.
In the next life I see you batting
At the noon-toiled flies in your eyes.
For now its jazz can up swat down woo-wee!
Just glinting like a moon-child,
Scooting like a scooter should.

PALM SUNDAY

A thought interrupts. A draggy river
Runs under a cloud of power.
There will be signs, all right. The Giver

Of time and anecdote splits the hour
Into years that hone
Their edges on the edges of a rumor.

Words wait to be filled, as if they could
Digest their meanings' absences
Without the call of being loved or understood.

And yet, even now, there is no sense
Which doesn't end in an unfolding
On the loud map of the soul. The miracle then?

The remote slate of a gravestone, sprinkling
The grass with pardons, or the skin
Seaming the scar of a knee into pink plastic?

The sea roars and tosses like a great plant
In ecstasy that warms the morning
And emerges eternally from an instant.

WAY AHEAD OF THE GAME

You open your hand, the sky darkens with verbiage.
You open your throat, the wound becomes ensouled.

Shoveling hope into your mouth
Like a planet-eating god,
You enter the cove of nothing, covet everything.

Soporific fumbles = a cold compress on eternity,
A straitjacket around immortal life.

■

A little stitch in a summer dress.
A little stitch in the girl in it.

■

I want your longitudes,
The crisp smell of your peroxide ears.
I want your seesaw over a burning canticle.

■

I'm told everyone is writing poems about stones.
Arborescent quarantine, I speak you only.

■

We roll our pennies,
We nickel and dime,
We spend a senseless morning in thrall
To that which we resemble
And so,

And so?
And so?

Surrender.

YOUR DEATH

Who is to say that all men
Are not amnesia-laden gods
Who carry their genius in bags,
That each sunrise will not bear

Envious celebration to your memory,
That you will not return to this world
Where steel is torn like paper from the earth
When I become a splinter in these winds?

The white winter light brands your initials
Across my eyelids, while the brilliant mahogany
Of your ringing footsteps echoes these karmic rustlings.
And the near exquisite lines

In your mother's aging face,
Your cabinets glinting with fresh vegetables,
The ocean's tongue spitting at your one window,
Are souvenirs that fall around my feet

Like the shards of sun
Shaken from the jagged tones of your hair.
It must get difficult,
All of this not wanting to die,

Harder than keeping up with the neighbors
Left prodding the twilight in fields.
Yet your own eyes fishing in the dark
Will persist: Again and again,

The ace of your misfortunes
Has not entailed a loss of respect
For objects within your field of dignity
As you remain perched on your lopsided shore

Now almost fully slicked with the radiant solace
Descending as patiently as a wing upon you.
You will persist,
And today I rinse myself completely

In your songs, in the passing time,
And leave you with your first two fingers
On the pulse of this late century,

And the disembodied thumb of the traveler
Who awaits you, in your new womb.

POEM FOR THE END OF TIME

for Damon Tomblin

My neighborhood   my neighborhood   my neighborhood
    Up in flames my neighborhood
On apocalypse waves of scalene dreams
I rode past in chariots across the valleys
Tore a hole in my destiny
It was weird and cold and dark there

My neighborhood   my neighborhood   my neighborhood
    Up in flames my neighborhood
The B on fire the R on fire the double O on fire like breasts
Pulled apart by burning clamps
K the K of The Trial and what have I done
The L the old empty El not carting back my grandfather
To his wife of a WWII grenade and shards of violins
The Y o Y Y Y did I look into those gypsy eyes
It was weird and cold and dark there
The N the N of my name singing

God is here God is here God is here
Singing may all my enemies go to hell
Noel Noel Noel Noel

My neighborhood   my neighborhood   my neighborhood
    Up in flames my neighborhood
There were jars turning black in my neighborhood
I saw smoke rising from them in my neighborhood
I was not stupid, my eyes were not blind
But Y o Y did I look back, pillar of Morton's salt
Why did I bend to taste the sodden grass of the soul
Why did I leave You to go to that place
It was weird and cold and dark there
The Holy Spirit was there but I could not see it
It was darkly blue shining but I could not see it

Gaze as reverently into another's eyes as if you were
Looking at the gates of hell Franz K says
As if standing before the gates of hell Kafka says

In my neighborhood I knocked at the gate
In my neighborhood the answer was yes
In my neighborhood I entered no longer an Innocent
In my neighborhood I became one of them one of them

No longer rinsed in the blue space of flames
I became one of them my neighborhood my neighborhood

Someone rides on a train in my neighborhood
Someone hangs off a fire escape in my neighborhood
The buildings sway ever so slightly in wind

The first time I left my neighborhood God wept
When I returned the sunsets were blood

My neighborhood   my neighborhood   my neighborhood
      Up in flames my neighborhood
The portal to my sixth sense pried open
The portal my sixth sense pride open and open
I don't think it will ever shut now

Opened and opened my neighborhood my neighborhood
Every second was a walking dream
Every minute was a talking spell
Every hour an apocalypse wave on a scalene dream

Now I'm rowing, rowing, the awful rowing
The rowing of penance the rowing through all its stages
I tore a hole in my destiny
I left You my destiny
It was weird and cold and dark there

My neighborhood   my neighborhood   my neighborhood
    Up in flames my neighborhood
Death is a master from Bensonhurst
Death is a master from Avenue M

A dog licks the sores of a century
Lazarus, Lazarus who will be the master of the house?
Who will be the dark funny gypsy whirling across
The scalene dreams of my apocalypse neighborhood

Telling my future to the laughing moon?
My innocence, where is it?
I tore a hole in my destiny

A whole in my destiny
My neighborhood   my neighborhood   my neighborhood
I brought you the Holy Spirit my neighborhood
On index cards I painted them blue my neighborhood
God smiled on my neighborhood
The Creator gave me a shot of His presence my neighborhood
So as to gratify my yearning for Him my neighborhood
Now go and do likewise my neighborhood my neighborhood

America your poets flock to my neighborhood
Your beautiful wounded birds to my neighborhood
Your Holy Spirits
My destiny wraps around me like a fence my neighborhood
A fence that I will never climb my neighborhood
Bells toll in my neighborhood
Books are burning in my neighborhood

Candles are used for fucking people in my neighborhood
Why did I bend to taste the sodden grass in my neighborhood
The scalene waves riding over the cemeteries
And we will have to get down on all 4s
And we will have to get down on all 4s
And we will have to get down on all 4s and eat those grasses
For ever and ever
Amen

In my neighborhood I dreamed of you as a child
I dreamed you sat on my bed smiling at me with a guitar
Damon Daemon Damiano
You were my fate
You were my fate
Our fate was joy
How to translate this
How to transpose it
How to transcend it
To transfigure it

Grasses grasses
Which blades to lick

My neighborhood   my neighborhood   my neighborhood
     Up in flames my neighborhood
In my neighborhood I dreamed of you as a child
O Viking man with a guitar
Hands of gold, hands of myrrh

Fingers full of blood and weeping
Fingers full of virgins and endless weeping
Weeping as Rachel weeps she will not be comforted
My neighborhood   my neighborhood   my neighborhood
     Up in flames my neighborhood
With my visions visions visions
Of skull shattered martyrs in Laramie, Wyoming
On a sunny afternoon

This crazy government my neighborhood
With its rituals and spells my neighborhood

With its gag laws and baptisms
With its Golden Gloves and Southern Comfort
Rising with phoenix, rising from ashes
Rising from governments
Rising from corporate blood
Trekking it across Indonesia
Trekking it across Brazil
Trekking it across Africa
Trekking it across Kosovo
Trekking it across Emerging Markets
God weeps in my neighborhood
The South Pole has moved 15 feet in the last year my neighborhood
The ice is melting, the penguins are weeping
God why do You abandon us here, here like this?

My neighborhood   my neighborhood   my neighborhood
     Up in flames my neighborhood
I call out to you who are living my neighborhood
I call out to you who live in my house my neighborhood
Where I walk around in my ghost shoes

Where I eat and drink rust
Where I roll in the grasses of cemeteries
Where the dead, the real dead of gag laws
Of Golden Gloves
Of Southern Comfort
Where they lie unconfined
Down into the memory
    Down into the memory
        Down into the memory and memory and memory
Down into the memory (kiss me)
You will go

My neighborhood   my neighborhood   my neighborhood
    Up in flames my neighborhood
Up into the penitential rite
Well-digger in the wind
Up into the yards on fire
Up into skeletons burning in bathrooms
Rattling a version of what was to come

In the stuff of weird and cold and dark
My life is an evil river in my neighborhood
My life is a penitential rite in my neighborhood
My life is the Holy Spirit in my neighborhood
My life is the Word bisected into time
My life is the Word bisected into flesh
Fruit of the vine and work of human hands
Unseen nightlong real

I wanted to see but I've seen too much
O Viking man
I did not go there as an Innocent this time
Meridian means circle of fire
Meridian the spirit who sang in my ear
Sang in my neighborhood in my ear in my sleep
On apocalypse waves of a scalene dream

My 17th birthday, first year in Edison, N.J., I received the following
    message about the end of the world:

5. The beasts shall fall through the chinks in the earth
4. Buildings will crumble
3. Possessions will begin to disappear
2. Crowds will become thinner
1. There will be a blinding light streaming through everything
    everything everything

I woke to the dread of my driver's test, and to a deer with tremendous antlers looking in at me from the patio. I did not know not to touch the glass. I did not know:

That the animal could shatter the glass and tear through the house
That the glass could shatter and tear my throat in scalene waves of
    apocalypse dreams

Meridian means circle of fire. I did not know this age 25 Gainesville, Florida, wolf-disease loping through my blood. I did not know this and I listened to her when she sang to me shrilly of dark salvation. I would have known I say I would have known but the week of my wedding I looked at the Holy Spirit through the eyes of

The Fool not knowing which road to take
The Magician and Priestess
Their offspring the Empress
The Emperor who is the number 4

But not the Holy Spirit Number 4
Not the Word made flesh Number 4
4   4   4   4 You are so good to me number 4
You are beautiful and radiant with great splendor number 4
So good to emit Your bluest light
Of Him most high, You bear the likeness
And no mortal lips are worthy to pronounce Your name
But You descended down into the memory
    Down into the memory
        Down into the memory (kiss me)
You would go
Into Sister Sleep Number 4
Into Brother Anxiety Number 4
Into Mother Hell and Father Lie
You descended number 4

It was weird and cold and dark there

My neighborhood   my neighborhood   my neighborhood

    Number 4 my neighborhood

America your poets are flocking to my neighborhood

They are sick of your insane demands my neighborhood

They take jobs at dry cleaners

They take jobs at Starbucks

They take jobs in editorial offices getting their asses pinched by

    washed-out Medeas

They take jobs cleaning the apartments of drug dealers

They take jobs that come with cellular phones

They accept vocations of Ultimate Holy Envy

(And why, dear friend, do you have to be the Messiah?

Couldn't you settle for Immanuel Kant,

O beautiful cerebral ever-virgin dragging yourself across the starry

    sky of non-self

With your sexy blue eyes and kindest heart?)

They take jobs licking the blood from the grasses of cemeteries

Sowing their seed in the whore of the Bloomberg

The seven-eyed monster of the binary code

The digital metempsychosis of why America, why must your Holy
    Spirits drink of your blood
You leave them no choice America
You leave them no choice America
But to drip their blood across energy and all its sectors

Across the monologic wind of their vexations
Across the Pistis, Elpis and Agape of machines
And the sacked altar of their mother Sophia
They drip holy blood from Aleph to Tau
Across scalene waves of your Real Presence
Of Golden Gloves and Southern Comfort
Your Miss Americas and battalion commanders turned defense
    plant presidents
You leave them no choice America
You leave them no choice America
And the dromedaries weep, they weep across a nation
Marking its head with a Tau with a Tau
Dripping blood over smiling caffeine-pickers in orientation films at
    Starbucks, USA

USA USA USA USA
The last card of the Major Arcana, The World
I flick the switch on you America
I want you to feel how it is to be S*H*O*C*K*E*D out of your body
To be fucked into oblivion
To be fucked into God-with-Us symbols of music on a page
What is this river of stars that runs through us all?

My neighborhood   my neighborhood   my neighborhood
      Up in flames my neighborhood
I've trekked my blood all over
From Ocean Avenue to Brooklyn Heights
From Coney Island to Far Rockaway
From the communion of saints to the forgiveness of sins
From Brother Sun to Sister Death
From Kierkegaard to Saint Michel
Queer bald altar boy in leather blessing us all
Blessing Folsome Street
Blessing the Castro
Blessing the Valley of Death

Blessing Japanese Zen
Blessing blessing blessing
Us all for 20 centuries of stony sleep
Blessing us and blessing us
Paris, America, your Holy Spirits
America Matthew Shepard is an angel weeping over us
Pierced by the Holy Spirit forever in heaven
America when will you hear my novenas
In smoke rising from jars
America the Creator has given me a shot of His presence
America I stand under Atlas

Dripping my blood across 5th Avenue
Dripping my blood on the walls of St. Pat's
America your beautiful birds
They flock to my neighborhood
O Viking man with a guitar
You sat on a bed in my neighborhood
You lay on a bed in my neighborhood
Viking man now I never see you anymore

In the night, the stars, the way things used to be
Why did I look into those gypsy eyes
It was weird and cold and dark there
Alone, alone, alone, alone with my visions of skull-shattered martyrs
In Laramie, Wyoming
America what is this river of stars that runs through us all?

My neighborhood   my neighborhood   my neighborhood
    Up in flames my neighborhood
Your skull-shattered martyrs your martyrs tied to fences and left for
    scarecrows
In Laramie, Wyoming
Wyoming of Pollock Wyoming of Guardians of the Secret
Wyoming of dogs licking a ritual
The totems are burning
The man has become numbers
The woman is an ocean and an eye

When I was 5 I was told there were giant vegetables who were trying
to kill me, perhaps most especially the giant tomato who would
pound on the door while 3 6s danced on my head. No one heard.

My 6th sense pried open I don't think it will stop
My 6th sense pride open I don't think it will stop
It is weird and cold and dark here
The gypsies are no longer funny
And I am no longer an Innocent

Bless me my neighborhood for I have sinned
I'm writing that poem from coast to coast
I'm singing that poem from coast to coast
Brother of Francis
I'm making my pilgrimage from Word to Thing
From Brooklyn Bridge to Golden Gate
From Posman Books to City Lights
From LUNGFULL! to 6500
From Fence to Zyzzyva
From LIT to God knows what they'll come up with next
From Clover to Rohrer
From to Stroffolino to Hillman
From young Fuhrman to the rocky fault
I'm singing my novenas 9 × 9
Coffins no alphabet can contain

Coffins no gag laws can contain
No Golden Gloves
No Southern Comfort
Damon Daemon Damiano
O God rebuild my Church
It is weird and cold and dark here
Which you can see is falling into ruins
It is weird and cold and dark here
America your saints are scarecrows
America your manifest destiny is Starbucks
America your frontiers are weeping Emerging Markets
America I make money from this
America I mark your head with a Tau with a Tau
Your bird, your Holy Spirit, yours truly (courtesy of Microsoft's
      Autotext)

America Be
            Righteous
            Over
            Our

Kingdom
Love
Your
Neighbor

America Mother Hell and Father Lie
Have poisoned all the apple pie
America I am the guardian of your secrets
I tore a hole in my destiny trying to understand you
And now I am no longer an Innocent
Bless me my neighborhood for I have sinned
Bless me for I have sinned against your Holy Spirit
Every second was a waking dream
Every minute was a walking spell
Brother of Francis pray for me
It is weird and cold and dark here
$45,000 in credit cards = $20 out of some CEO's pocket
The gypsies are no longer funny my neighborhood
And I am no longer an Innocent my neighborhood
What a feral fucked-up riff on the Walden experiment
    my neighborhood

But you see I wished to live deliberately my neighborhood
To front only the essential facts of life my neighborhood
And see if I could not learn what it had to teach my neighborhood
And not, when I came time to die, discover I had not lived my
    neighborhood
And my eyes were no longer blind

In my neighborhood I knocked at the gate
In my neighborhood the answer was yes
In my neighborhood I am no longer an Innocent
In my neighborhood I became one of them one of them

You leave me no choice my neighborhood
You leave me no choice my neighborhood
Dripping my blood across scalene dreams
Eating the grasses of the cemeteries on all 4s
With you ever-virgin-cum-Messiah of sexy blue eyes and kindest heart
Couldn't you just be Immanuel Kant?
It was weird and cold and dark with you
In Sister Sleep

In Brother Anxiety
In Mother Hell and Father Lie
When I listened to Meridian sing shrilly of dark salvation
Now my life is a penitential rite
My life tears through my house like a word-deer through a forest
I did not know not to touch the glass
My life is a penitential rite in my neighborhood
My life is the Holy Spirit bisected into time into flesh
What is this river of stars that runs through us all?

Viking man I stand under Atlas
Dripping my novenas on the walls of St. Pat's
America your birds flock to my neighborhood
America your Holy Spirits flock to my neighborhood
Viking man with a guitar
You sat on my bed in my neighborhood
You lay on my bed in my neighborhood
O why did I look into those gypsy eyes
Death is a master from Bensonhurst
Death is a master from Avenue M

Alone alone with my visions of skull-shattered martyrs
Alone in black smoke rising from jars
My neighborhood I tore a hole in my destiny
My neighborhood of beautiful birds
My neighborhood of hidden cemeteries
My neighborhood of ghost shoes of Bloomberg and blood
My neighborhood gleaming with Brother Sun
Now even He is killing us too
My neighborhood someone wants to jab a Coke billboard
Through the fair face of Sister Moon

America your skull-shattered martyrs
Are fucked into the God-symbols of music
Are fucked into Emerging Markets
Are fucked into your frontiers slouching toward the rough beast
    of Bloomberg
Are fucked into Irony
Are fucked into your genetically-altered apple pie
I tore a hole in my destiny trying to understand you
O why did I ruin myself Brother of Francis

Why did I ruin myself I've seen too much
A bell tolled in my neighborhood
Books rose from the flames in my neighborhood
A candle fucked someone in my neighborhood
God please rebuild my Church my neighborhood
As you can see I am falling into ruins my neighborhood
I sing shrilly of dark salvation
I sing shrilly of essences
I sing of Douglas firs burning in the moonlight of Twin Peaks
They are burning over the Black Lodge set my people free
Come to us Emmanuel, not on a lawnmower riding over the lost
    highways of collapsed daylight
Not with Lula and Sailor riding into the desert
Past accidents, past blood, past tongues of backward speech
Past the raped bodies of homecoming queens she's dead wrapped
    in plastic
Past the body of a virgin washed over by ocean dross
Over a face drawn in sand at the edge of a sea
Alone with my visions of skull-shattered martyrs
I call out to you my love

I sing in the shower to you my love

I turn on all the lights my love

I kiss your beautiful wounded hands my love

Your hands full of virgins, your hands full of blood

How to understand it, how to translate it

Brother of Francis I've seen too much

In my neighborhood I spoke in the tongues of angels

In my neighborhood I spoke in the tongues of men

In my neighborhood a gong resounded

In my neighborhood a cymbal clanged

A bell tolled, a book slammed shut, a candle sputtered out its last

I tore a hole in my destiny

Now I hang in a field of blood

Brother of Francis pray for me

Go fuck yourself with your 30 pieces of silver my neighborhood

Shove it up your God-damned ass my neighborhood

I eat you like a tiger of shame

Like a little girl a tiger of shame

The rain is falling now on these words my neighborhood

Staining these pages as I write my neighborhood

And I've written that the baptism of the insider is a lettered feat
And I've written that the great god Dionysus tore the babes
From their mothers' wombs and made them suckle
The firewater instead of the breast
And I've written that he whipped them with the purple vines
And with the purple vines he baptized them
I wrote those words after I left my neighborhood
After I was forcepted a second time at 15 from your womb my
    neighborhood
Now I am speaking these words smearing their black love across
    the warm winter rain my neighborhood
I am speaking these words and you can't stop me my neighborhood
The wind is blowing fiercely my neighborhood
I sing shrilly of dark salvation
I sing poems in self-help books
I sing sunsets
I sing sunsets
I sing Irony into the skull-shattered walls of oblivion
I sing Bloomberg
I sing blood

My neighborhood what did you do to your Holy Spirits
They are raped by the candles of Irony my neighborhood
The bells are tolling my neighborhood
The books are filling up with resounding cymbals my neighborhood
I lift up my candle my neighborhood
The rain is falling even harder my neighborhood
I am speaking this poem as I'm writing it my neighborhood
People are walking by wondering what I'm doing my neighborhood
When they ask I ask them to bless me my neighborhood
The last man said he would bless everyone my neighborhood
In this river of stars that runs through us all my neighborhood
I will ride over scalene dreams in a paper boat my neighborhood
My words will rise like phoenixes my neighborhood
Alone, alone, alone, alone
From Ocean Avenue to Brooklyn Heights
From Coney Island to Far Rockaway
From Brooklyn Bridge to Golden Gate
From the communion of saints to the forgiveness of sins
And Irony is the most wounded bird of all my neighborhood
Her wings are painted black my neighborhood

She covers her knees with a shawl my neighborhood

She rocks back and forth in the dusk my neighborhood

Perhaps some raggedy sense will in fact sneak back into our lives
my neighborhood

Irony is the most wounded bird of all my neighborhood

She speaks like Diane Sawyer yet she is a Jedi Knight my
neighborhood

She rocks back and forth and cries all alone my neighborhood

20 Centuries of stony sleep my neighborhood

And we will have to get down on all 4s and eat the grasses of them all

Saint Michel queer altar boy in leather blessing us blessing us

Blessing us from Folsome Street

Blessing us from the Castro

Blessing us from Japanese Zen

Blessing us from Paris

Blessing us in a chador

Blessing us in hospices

Blessing us all your Holy Spirit

We climb past midnight my neighborhood

We climb past Kafka my neighborhood

We climb past literary theory my neighborhood

Where Baudrillard proves the Gulf War never happened my
neighborhood

Where the starving bodies of Iraqi children disappear without a
trace my neighborhood

Into signifiers dancing like bloody hooks my neighborhood

They are the well-diggers in the wind my neighborhood

We rise up past our yards on fire my neighborhood

Yards full of ears and skeletons in bathrooms my neighborhood

This is the stuff of revolution my neighborhood

It has been light-sabered into your skull-shattered martyrs my
neighborhood

Your dead lay their hands on us in absolution my neighborhood

Your Holy Spirits, your birds shitting their Todesworten across
the grasses of a century my neighborhood

Achtung my neighborhood

Achtung my neighborhood

I tore a hole in my destiny

I drip blood on your Church walls

I sing my novenas from smoky black jars

And the movies that eke past the death machine

And the movie where the oracle says, maybe you'll remember that
    you don't really believe in any of that fate crap

Do you

Neo

Neo

Well, my neighborhood, neither do I believe in any of that fate crap

Brother of Francis pray for me

While I lift up my candle over my apocalypse dreams

The Word will cross the forest like a gazelle

And bisect itself into time once again

Bless me Father for I have sinned

Bless me Brother of Francis for I have sinned

Bless me Viking Man for I have sinned

Bless me Kind Virgin with sexy blue eyes for I have sinned

Bless me my neighborhood for I have sinned

Bless me again with your beach chairs and trees

Your yentas and supermarkets
Your invisible bookstores and handball courts
And Brother Sun who is so radiant
And Sister Moon who is so fair
And your birds who see fit to graze my hair
Go now and sin no more my neighborhood
But always remember my neighborhood my neighborhood
Remember the black jars and stony sleep
Remember the visions of skull-shattered martyrs
The apocalypse boats of scalene dreams
Remember the rowing of penance, the rowing through all its stages
Remember the tearing of holes in destiny
Remember the squares that were darkly blue shining
And sunsets of blood
Remember well-digger in the wind
Remember the signifiers clinging to us like bloody hooks
Remember the skeletons rattling bathrooms
Remember the forests full of suffixes
Remember in the bosom of Mother Hell, on the shoulders of
    Father Lie

Remember the B on fire the R on fire
The double O pried apart by burning clamps
Remember the K of the K of The Trial and what have I done
Remember the low murmurs in L-shaped rooms
The Y Y Y asked of the Once-He-was-washing-the-world
One and Infinite, annihilated, —ied
Remember the N of God is here God is here
Remember that light was
Salvation
Remember your Holy Spirits
In all that is seen and unseen
Remember in Hatred, Injury, Doubt, Despair, Darkness, Sadness
    and their dear sister Irony
Who is the most wounded bird of all
Who weeps in secret in her raggedy shawl
Remember your birds grazing each other's hair
From Ocean Avenue to Brooklyn Heights
From Coney Island to Far Rockaway
From Posman Books to City Lights
From Brooklyn Bridge to Golden Gate

From Brother Sun to Sister Death
From Paris to NYC
From Indonesia to Brazil
From Africa to Kosovo
From Alpha to Omega
From Aleph to Tau
Tau marking our heads where we weep without ceasing
Remember the low murmurs in L-shaped rooms
Remember in Hatred, Injury, Doubt, Despair, Darkness, Sadness
    and their dear sister Irony
Remember through the tearing of holes in destiny
Remember the 4s that were darkly blue shining
Remember the sunsets full of blood full of blood
Remember that the Creator loves us very much
And that the Creator has given us a shot of His presence
And that we are stars in the same endless river
I lift up my candle my neighborhood
I call out to you my neighborhood
I sing in the shower to you my neighborhood
I turn on all the lights my neighborhood

For this we were given a voice my neighborhood
For this we were given a voice my neighborhood
For this   for this   for this   and for this
For this we were given a voice
My neighborhood   my neighborhood   my neighborhood